THE OFFICIAL
QUEENS PARK RANGERS
ANNUAL 2010

A Grange Publication

Written by Francis Atkinson & Ian Taylor

Designed by Colin Heggie

© 2009. Published by Grange Communications Ltd., Edinburgh, under licence from Queens Park Rangers Football Club. Printed in the EU.

Photography © Action Images

ISBN 978-1-906211-86-8

£6.99

CONTENTS

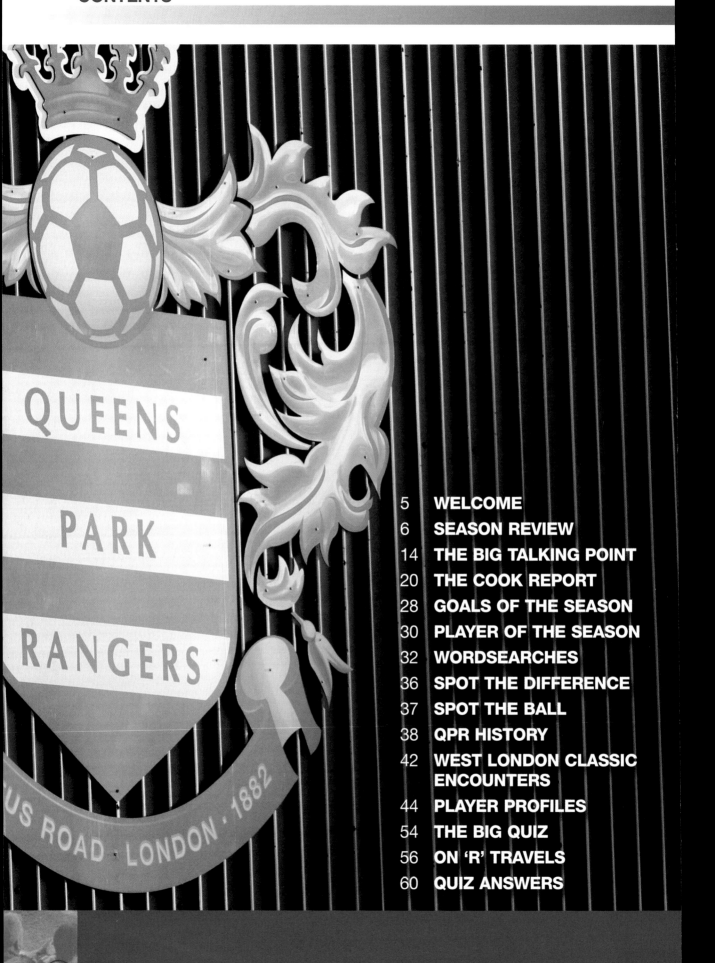

WELCOME

Welcome to The Official Queens Park Rangers Annual 2010

The 2008/09 campaign was certainly eventful for everyone associated to the Super Hoops.

Our memorable Carling Cup victory against Aston Villa was the undoubted highlight, and it was little surprise to anyone to see the goalscorer in that victory – Damion Stewart – crown an outstanding personal season by scooping both the Player's Player and Supporter's Player of the Year awards.

Indeed, it was very much a case for the defence in the end of season honours, with Matthew Connolly receiving the Young Player of the Year gong for a series of committed and equally efficient displays across the backline throughout the duration of the season.

In the following pages, you will find a comprehensive review of the season, as well as an in-depth look at the players who wore the famous Blue and White Hoops with such distinction throughout the last 12 months.

There are also quizzes and posters and much, much more - so read on and enjoy!

Come on you R's!

Francis Atkinson & Ian Taylor

SEASON REVIEW

AUGUST

Fitz Hall scored twice and missed a second half spot-kick, as Iain Dowie's new-look QPR opened the 2008/09 Coca-Cola Championship campaign with a comeback victory against Barnsley.

Trailing to Iain Hume's fifth minute goal, Rangers scored twice in as many minutes to stun the visitors from South Yorkshire.

Hall poked home from close range in the 29th minute, before notching an early contender for goal of the season a minute later, with an extraordinary volley.

Hall squandered a golden chance for a hat-trick when he fluffed his lines from the spot after Dexter Blackstock was felled in the box, before Barnsley were reduced to ten men when Marciano Van Homoet was sent off.

Rangers booked their place in the next round of the Carling Cup, with a hard-fought yet fully deserved win over a spirited Swindon Town.

Goals from Angelo Balanta, Dexter Blackstock and Damien Delaney saw Iain Dowie's men advance to round two at the expense of the League One outfit.

To their credit though, Maurice Malpas' side competed valiantly throughout and had led 2-1 at one stage, thanks to goals from Simon Cox and Billy Paynter.

QPR's fairytale start to the season came to a shuddering halt with a 3-0 defeat at a noisy Bramall Lane.

Ex-Scunthorpe striker Billy Sharp did the damage with a marvellous hat-trick, as Iain Dowie's side failed to use the momentum gained from last weekend.

QPR did the memory of Ray Jones proud with an impressive 2-0 win over South Yorkshire side Doncaster Rovers.

Dexter Blackstock and a first strike for Argentine Emmanuel Ledesma sealed all three points for the R's who banished memories of last Saturday's 3-0 defeat at Sheffield United with an assured performance full to the brim of attacking flair and creative genius.

The game marked the year anniversary of the death of striker Jones who was tragically killed in a car accident, and a tribute was played on the new giant screen to remember one of the Club's most promising players.

A scintillating hat-trick from midfielder Emmanuel Ledesma capped off a stunning 4-0 victory over League One side Carlisle United.

Rangers left the field to a standing ovation, richly deserved after a performance that blew

away the Cumbrian outfit with four goals of the highest quality.

Almost forgotten amidst Ledesma's remarkable achievement, was the opening goal from Damion Stewart, before the midfielder grabbed the limelight with both hands and took away the match ball.

QPR battled to a well-earned point against Bristol City despite having Emmanuel Ledesma controversially sent off.

Dexter Blackstock's early strike was cancelled out by Dele Adebola, but despite the second half dismissal of Argentine Ledesma, Rangers held firm for their first away point of the season.

SEPTEMBER

Dexter Blackstock was tormentor-in-chief as the ex-Southampton striker's brace, accompanied by goals from Damion Stewart and Patrick Agyemang, sent QPR to fourth in the Championship table, after a hard fought 4-1 victory over the South Coast side.

Blackstock opened the scoring with not even a minute on the clock, only for Adam Lallana to bring the scores level. Stewart then prodded the home side ahead once more, with Blackstock adding his side's third, and his second, with a cool finish with quarter of an hour left to play, before Agyemang scored his first goal of the season.

Ten-man QPR defied the odds to snatch a fully deserved 1-0 victory over Norwich City at Carrow Road.

Captain Marvel Martin Rowlands earned the win with a fine free-kick for his first of the campaign, after the R's had earlier been reduced to ten men following Matt Connolly's double booking.

QPR's impressive start to the season suffered its latest setback as - despite dominating the second half - Elliott Ward's first half penalty gave Coventry City all three points.

Mikele Leigertwood's foul on Sky Blues midfielder Jay Tabb gave the home side the chance from 12-yards, which Ward converted to ensure Manager Iain Dowie's return to The Ricoh Arena was not as he had hoped.

Damion Stewart's second half header booked Rangers' place in the Fourth Round of the Carling Cup, on a night to remember for Iain Dowie's side.

The Jamaican international leapt to head home Daniel Parejo's pin-point cross, as the R's - backed by 2,500 fanatical fans - claimed the notable scalp of a Villa side currently sitting pretty in fourth spot in the Premiership.

Victory was no less than the R's deserved, as Villa failed to breakdown a resolute Rangers defence.

QPR suffered from a League Cup hangover after Martin Albrechtsen's volley and Emanuel Villa's header gave Derby County all three points at Loftus Road.

After the dramatic night at Villa Park midweek, Rangers players gave a frustrating performance in front of a boisterous home support.

Dexter Blackstock spared QPR blushes as his header cancelled out Gary Taylor-Fletcher's opener as Rangers drew at Loftus Road with a spirited Blackpool.

Despite a host of chances for the home side, Iain Dowie's men could not find a winner against a determined Tangerines outfit.

OCTOBER

Birmingham City striker Kevin Phillips gave a master-class in forward play, as his goal saw off an out-of-sorts QPR at St Andrews.

Sporting the new red away kit for the very first time, the R's never really looked like scoring and fell behind to Phillips's strike on the stroke of half-time from Garry O'Connor's pass.

QPR had Akos Buzsaky to thank for restoring that winning feeling to Loftus Road, after the Hungarian midfield maestro scored a stunning goal to steal maximum points from a battling Nottingham Forest.

Youngster Angelo Balanta had given the R's the lead minutes into the second half, before Buzsaky drilled a fine shot beyond visiting keeper Paul Smith to double the Hoops' advantage.

Forest hit back through Lewis McGugan's perfectly taken free-kick, but Rangers held on to claim a very welcome three points.

QPR were fortunate to come away with a point against an imperious Swansea City side at the Liberty Stadium, as a heated exchange ended in a 0-0 stalemate.

The game was marred by a nasty looking injury to home keeper Dorus de Vries after an accidental collision with Martin Rowlands.

QPR battled to a well-earned point against a Reading side that had not dropped a single point at the Madejski Stadium.

In a game of few chances, but exciting nonetheless, Rangers had Radek Cerny and Damion Stewart to thank for keeping them in it as the Czech keeper made a brilliant save to deny home sub Kalifa Cisse, whilst Jamaican Stewart was a colossus throughout.

Ten-man QPR produced a memorable display that is destined for the archives after grinding out a stunning 1-0 win over high-flying Birmingham City.

Samuel Di Carmine was the hero of the night after his bullet strike on 54 minutes raised the roof off Loftus Road and inspired a performance worthy of caretaker Manager Gareth Ainsworth.

Even when Mikele Leigertwood was controversially sent off on the stroke of half-time, the R's battled hard and were worthy of the victory.

NOVEMBER

QPR's four-match unbeaten run ground to a shuddering halt, as super-sub Jon Stead scored twice in four second half minutes at a wet and windy Portman Road.

The former Sunderland and Sheffield United

striker bundled home his first on 71 minutes, then coolly headed a second from an Owen Garvan corner three minutes later.

Substitute Gavin Mahon's 80th minute header won it for the R's, as nine-man Cardiff City returned to Wales pointless.

The experienced midfield general rose to head home Peter Ramage's back post cross, as Rangers moved level on points with the Welsh outfit in the Championship table.

QPR exited the Carling Cup after going down 1-0 at a drenched Old Trafford after a Carlos Tevez penalty condemned the R's to a long homeward journey.

In truth, the visitors never really threatened and were largely outplayed by their more illustrious hosts.

The R's put on a gutsy, determined defensive showing, with keeper Radek Cerny in sparkling form throughout to deny a host of United players.

Burnley substitute Alan Mahon's well-taken goal stole the points in an entertaining encounter at Loftus Road.

Dexter Blackstock's driven shot flew by visiting keeper Brian Jensen to hand the R's the lead as early as the 14th minute, but Burnley hit back just after the half hour mark, as Robbie Blake smashed home from the edge of the box.

Substitute Mahon, on for the injured Chris Eagles, then won it for Burnley seconds before the hour.

QPR began their London derby trilogy with a disappointing 3-0 defeat at the hands of a resurgent Watford side.

In a match in which Rangers never got going, goals from Tommy Smith, Darren Ward and Lee Williamson meant the R's went home pointless.

Dexter Blackstock struck twice in either half to hand new QPR boss Paulo Sousa a first win in his first match at Loftus Road.

The ex-Southampton marksman smashed home the match's opener on 17 minutes after good work from Damiano Tommasi, before Therry Racon brought the scores level, thundering home from close range after a fine Charlton move.

But Blackstock lifted the roof off Loftus Road in the 79th minute, as he rose majestically to head over a despairing Nicky Weaver to give Sousa a first win, and Rangers a vital three points.

QPR finished their London derby trilogy by holding Crystal Palace to an uninspiring 0-0 draw at a wet and cold Selhurst Park.

In a game of few chances, the match was summed up by new striker Heidar Helguson missing an open goal, and the R's testing home keeper Julian Speroni just once through Patrick Agyemang.

DECEMBER

QPR graced the Sky Sports cameras with a wonderful display of attacking football that blew away Championship pace-setters Wolverhampton Wanderers.

Martin Rowlands' second goal of the season just

past the hour mark gave the R's a 1-0 victory, but Radek Cerny was the hero after three fantastic saves denied Wolves a ninth straight win.

QPR missed not only a hatful of chances, but ultimately the opportunity to break into the top-six, as they went down to a Leon Clarke goal on a bitingly cold night at Hillsborough.

Heidar Helguson, Patrick Agyemang and Lee Cook all saw efforts fail to make the breakthrough as the Owls weathered the storm and punished Rangers in the 74th minute.

QPR had to make do with a point at Plymouth Argyle, after substitute Steve MacLean's late goal for the hosts served to cancel out Heidar Helguson's opener.

The Bolton striker - currently on loan at Loftus Road - struck on 16 minutes to not only open his account for the R's, but also end a frustrating run of eight away matches without a goal.

Dexter Blackstock rose from the bench to nod home a late winner, after Rangers had twice relinquished the lead to high-flying Preston North End.

In a topsy-turvy encounter, Heidar Helguson headed home an early opener, only for Chris Sedgwick to restore parity with a header of his own.

After an Agyemang header fell kindly for the Iceland international to bundle home his and Rangers' second, Referee Alan Wiley plunged the match into controversy by awarding a contentious penalty that Callum Davidson duly thundered home.

Not to be outdone, Rangers threw everything forward in search of a winner and more than deserved to snatch victory thanks to Blackstock's headed goal.

QPR found themselves up against a stubborn Charlton Athletic side and had to make do with a point, as they crossed London to the Valley for the Boxing Day clash with the Addicks.

Rangers twice let go of the initiative as first Lee Cook curled a wonderful free-kick beyond Rob Elliot, only for Nicky Bailey to draw the scores level minutes into the second half.

Dexter Blackstock gave the R's a deserved lead on 68 minutes, but Bailey added his and Charlton's second with ten minutes remaining to give the Addicks a share of the spoils.

Rangers had to make do with a point as a determined Watford side held them to a goalless draw at a bitingly cold Loftus Road.

In an attempt to gain a measure of revenge for the 3-0 defeat at Vicarage Road earlier in the season, the R's went close through substitute Dexter Blackstock and Patrick Agyemang, whilst the visitors saw Lee Williamson strike a post with a curling free-kick.

JANUARY

After a goalless draw against Burnley in the FA Cup third round, QPR had to settle for a point against a determined Coventry City, who were reduced to ten men after 36 minutes when Stephen Wright saw red for a crude tackle on Heidar Helguson.

Despite the R's dominating proceedings, a Danny Fox free-kick handed the Sky Blues the lead after 72 minutes, before Dexter Blackstock bravely rose to nod over the onrushing Coventry keeper to hand Rangers a share of the points.

Burnley substitute Jay Rodriguez sent QPR crashing out of the FA Cup with a last minute goal in extra time.

The Clarets super-sub prolonged the R's third round misery, with a toe-poked finish in the dying seconds at Turf Moor.

Earlier, Steven Thompson cancelled out Samuel Di Carmine's opening strike in the 54th minute when he bundled home from close range, with both sides passing up glorious chances to snatch victory.

QPR finally broke their away day hoodoo with a well deserved win over Derby County at Pride Park.

Wayne Routledge opened the scoring with a fine placed finish to notch his first ever goal in a Rangers shirt and the outstanding Mikele Leigertwood grabbed himself the R's second in the 36th minute.

Heidar Helguson bagged a brace and Hogan Ephraim notched a late third, as Rangers chalked up a vital victory against Blackpool.

The Icelandic international bagged a goal in each half, the second from the penalty spot, before Ephraim capped a vintage away day with a third in added time.

In front of a season's highest attendance of 17,120, QPR extended their unbeaten run to

eight matches with a closely-fought draw with high-flying Reading.

For the second time in the season, the free-scoring Royals - English football's highest scorers - failed to find a way past the R's.

FEBRUARY

Rangers stretched their unbeaten run to nine matches with a hard-fought 2-2 draw with a resurgent Nottingham Forest.

Matteo Alberti proved the hero, despite giving away the first half penalty that Lewis McGugan converted, equalising with the last kick of the first 45 minutes.

Seconds into the second period and he doubled his and Rangers' tally for the day with a fine run and a cool finish to give the travelling R's fans something to shout about.

However, the win was not to be, as Chris Cohen rose unchallenged midway through the second period to guide home the leveller.

Despite grafting hard and playing some fine free-flowing football, QPR went down fighting 3-1 to an impressive Ipswich Town side.

Even when Jon Stead cancelled out Samuel Di Carmine's third minute opener, Rangers looked the most likely to earn the points, but Pablo Counago scored on the hour to put the visitors ahead.

With the R's pushing for an equaliser, Jon Walters added a third to steal the points away from the men in Hoops, who only looked like adding to their solitary goal through Mikele

11

Leigertwood's long-range strike and a Dexter Blackstock header late on.

An entertaining clash between two good footballing sides ended in a 0-0 stalemate, as Cardiff City battled a Queens Park Rangers side eager to continue their fine form on the road.

Heidar Helguson had the best opportunity of the match, connecting with Mikele Leigertwood's fine cross, but could only steer his effort wide from eight yards.

In an evenly-matched contest, a resilient Barnsley side narrowly stole the points against an equally as hard-working QPR side.

In a match of few chances, Rangers could count themselves unlucky not to return south with at least a point, after Damien Delaney cancelled out an early Daniel Bogdanovic header. But Anderson de Silva fired home from close range to give the Reds a somewhat fortuitous win.

MARCH

In tricky conditions, a hard-working and dominant QPR were undone by a moment of misfortune as Darel Russell's goal handed Norwich City all three points.

Controlling throughout, the R's created a host of chances, but could not apply the final touches to some brilliant passing moves and slick attacking play.

In an entertaining contest, QPR produced a display of real spirit and heart, coupled with fine attacking flair, to hold a lacklustre Sheffield United.

Dexter Blackstock and Matteo Alberti had the best chances for the home side. The striker nodding wide when well-placed only a few feet out, whilst the Italian midfielder blasted over with only the keeper to beat from ten yards.

Doncaster Rovers moved level on points with the R's in the Coca-Cola Championship table courtesy of a 2-0 win at The Keepmoat Stadium.

A Damion Stewart own goal and Paul Heffernan's close range header sealed it for the hosts, who continued their fine home form against a Rangers side, who for all their endeavours, failed to find a way past Rovers custodian Neil Sullivan.

In a resilient defensive display, coupled with some fine offensive guile, QPR found themselves somewhat out of luck when faced with a Southampton side battling relegation.

Most of the attacking play was done by the men in Hoops, with Hogan Ephraim, new-boy Adel Taarabt and Mikele Leigertwood all having efforts well saved or narrowly missing the target.

A bullet header from Mikele Leigertwood meant QPR returned to winning ways as they impressively triumphed over a spirited Swansea City side at Loftus Road.

Jordi López's beautifully taken free-kick on the half hour found the airborne skipper who arrowed a header into the far corner to hand Rangers their first win in 10 matches.

Rangers made it two wins in a week, with a thoroughly deserved 2-1 victory over fellow promotion hopefuls Bristol City.

In the 65th minute, Jordi López struck from 25 yards with a wonderful free-kick for his first Rangers goal, but when Michael McIndoe smashed home a leveller 12 minutes later it looked like a draw was in the offing.

But Rangers refused to be deterred in their quest for the points, and after Damien Delaney went on a lung-busting run down the left, his cross fell perfectly for Adel Taarabt to sweep home and send R's fans into raptures.

APRIL

QPR extended their unbeaten run and mini-revival with a goalless draw at home to Crystal Palace.

As the sun shone, Rangers controlled proceedings but were guilty of missing several chances, most notably in the second half, when Adel Taarabt broke free of the Eagles

defence only to blast an effort over the bar with only Julian Speroni to beat.

Part Four this season of Queens Park Rangers versus Burnley ended in a narrow 1-0 defeat for the Super Hoops as a towering header from R's old boy Clarke Carlisle condemned Gareth Ainsworth to defeat in his first match back at the helm.

QPR produced a spirited, determined display, coupled with some sensational attacking football to come back from two goals down to record an astonishing 3-2 win over Sheffield Wednesday.

After first Gavin Mahon had put the ball past his own keeper, and Marcus Tudgay added a penalty early in the second half, it seemed like all the hard work had been for nothing.

But Rowan Vine tapped home from close range to spark a remarkable comeback from the R's as Mahon atoned for his earlier mistake with the leveller with a brave diving header, and Damion Stewart blew the roof off Loftus Road with a late, late winner, nodding in a Lee Cook cross.

Failing in their quest to postpone Wolverhampton Wanderers' promotion party, QPR succumbed to a 1-0 defeat in the sunshine at Molineux.

Sylvan Ebanks-Blake scored the goal that takes Wolves to

the Premiership, after an uncharacteristic mistake from Damion Stewart, but the R's battled well and could've snatched an equaliser had Heidar Helguson picked his spot a little more carefully.

The last match of the season at Loftus Road ended in a 0-0 stalemate, as QPR made Plymouth Argyle wait until the final fixture of the season for survival.

MAY

An incredibly spirited QPR went down 2-1 at Preston on the final day of the season, as the hosts gate-crashed the play-offs at the expense of Cardiff City.

In a frantic match from start to finish, the hosts drew first blood through Jon Parkin just before the break, but ex-Lilywhite Patrick Agyemang drew matters level early in the second half with his second goal of the season. As the game wore on, the hosts pushed for an oh-so-crucial second and it came with 16 minutes to spare from Sean St Ledger.

THE BIG TALKING POINT

WHY DO THE FAMOUS BLUE AND WHITE HOOPS MAKE QPR FANS GO 'HOOPING' MAD?

We hit the streets of West London to get the answer, in this, the 50th successive year of the famous Blue and White Hoops.

When the first ball of the new season was kicked on Saturday 8th August, it marked the 50th successive year that QPR have worn the world famous Blue and White Hooped shirts.

And the fact Rangers did so wearing arguably one of the most stylish kits unveiled by the Club in recent years only serves to add weight to the claim that the iconic Hoops are now destined to go down in footballing folklore, both at home and abroad.

Ask any football fan - be they R's supporters or just ardent followers of the beautiful game - what their stand out image of Queens Park Rangers Football Club is, and for the lion's share, the answer will inevitably revolve around the Blue and White Hoops.

Worn by such greats as Rodney Marsh, Stan Bowles, Gerry Francis, Les Ferdinand, and in more recent times, Kevin Gallen and Lee Cook, the Hoops are legendary in these parts - as we found out by going on to the streets of West London to gauge the views of a quartet of QPR nuts.

Dave Robinson, a QPR supporter of 24 years, was bullish in his assessment.

"The Hoops are symbolic of QPR as we are the only team in England, if not Europe, that wear the famous Blue and White Hoops - and I include Reading in that! They have had a mixture of kits over the years and for that reason cannot be classed as real Hoops.

"Although we're not the most successful of English Clubs in terms of honours, we are one of the most famous, as we have a proud and illustrious history which dates back 127 years.

"Whenever I'm on holiday, in any part of the world, I am always sure to be recognised as a QPR fan when wearing the famous Hoops. This so called small Club from West London that has punched above its weight for so many years is alive and strong."

He added: "The Club and its fan base are from a tough working class area of West London. These are proud people and people who are even prouder of their Football Club.

"Queens Park Rangers Football Club gives them an identity and the famous Blue and White Hoops gives QPR its identity."

Matthew Webb, 21, believes the Hoops represent three important factors about the Club, namely its history, flair and community value.

"Many teams have altered the design of their shirts over the years, and in our early stages of life, Rangers were no different," he said.

"However, it's those famous Blue and White Hoops that have been our trademark for the most of the Club's existence and how symbolic they truly are.

"Not only do the Hoops make for one of the most fashionable team strips in football, their constant association with the Rangers name means they represent three important factors.

"History - they represent a side with a great tradition and history, a team that is amongst the oldest in The Football League and has previously spent many years among the top-flights elite with a brand of free-flowing and classy football.

"Flair - they show a Club who have become accustomed to embracing showman-type footballers. A team that has fashioned the likes of Rodney Marsh, Stan Bowles, Gerry Francis, and in more recent times, Trevor Sinclair, Lee Cook and Akos Buzsaky.

"Community - most importantly, they are emblematic of the community values. They are representative of a Club that lives and breathes because of its local community, a symbol of unity that saw the Club and its supporters fight off the bad times to move Rangers on to bigger and better things. And although we aren't the biggest Club, our togetherness is an exclusivity that is missing from so many others.

"The Hoops, for me, make us all proud because they represent a terrific history and indeed hopefully, a prosperous future."

For Sarah Holt, aged 36, the Hoops are 'instantly recognisable' as QPR, as she explained.

"With other Football Clubs, a block colour of red or blue or whatever it might be, could be any number of Clubs, but the Hoops can only be the R's.

"Football shirts change over the years - shades of colour, cut, design etc, but the R's will always be the Super Hoops regardless of designers' new ideas. No other Club can say that."

She added: "The first shirt I ever bought was the Guinness top, which is still regarded as a classic amongst the fans.

"And as with most kids, your favourite team influences other choices you make. My favourite of the Mr Men when I was young was Mr Bump, as he looked like a Rangers shirt!

"Tesco's was always the best shop too, because their carrier bags were blue and white. I even dressed our dog in one on the day of the '86 Cup Final!"

Fellow R's fan Gobi Ranganathan never went quite that far, but loves the fact that the R's stand out above all others - thanks to the famous Blue and White Hoops.

"The Blue and White Hoops are special," he said.

"They stand out from so many other teams' kits. You can spot someone wearing the colours in a crowd of people a mile away. And once you get each other's attention, there's an instant sense of belonging and mutual understanding of what we go through as R's fans."

It's views like these and so many others that not only make you proud to don the famous Blue and White Hoops, but also make you proud to be a QPR supporter.

And long may that continue...

HEIDAR HELGUSON

THE COOK
REPORT

LEE COOK EXCLUSIVE INTERVIEW BY IAN TAYLOR

A Rangers fan born and bred, Lee Cook lives and breathes Queens Park Rangers Football Club and the passion with which he speaks about the Club he loves never ceases to amaze.

On this occasion, it's the subject of the new home kit for the 2009/10 campaign that's getting his juices flowing.

"It's top quality isn't it," said Cook.

"The Blue and White Hoops are legendary. The lads are big fans of the white shorts too, but I'm not sure Cat, our Kit Man, feels the same!

"I grew up with them though, so from a personal viewpoint, I'm delighted they've brought them back."

Cook added: "It's got a really nice feel to it too.

"The people at Lotto and the Club have done a really good job with the design."

"

**The
Blue
and
White
Hoops
are
legendary**

"

"

"Of course it's all about the Hoops when it comes to QPR, but I think from a player's perspective, it's just as important that we feel comfortable in it and that's certainly the case with this new kit."

Having grown up in an era when the R's were flying high towards the summit of the top tier, Cook is more determined than most to see the Club he followed as a boy return to the Promised Land of the Premier League.

And whilst the R's missed out last season, Cook is realistic enough to acknowledge that the 2009/10 campaign promises to be 'the one', in the second full season since the arrival of Flavio Briatore, Bernie Ecclestone and co.

"We believe we can do it," said Cook.
"The reality is that this year has the potential to be the big one."

Cook, for one, has more reasons than most to dream about playing in the Premier League for the Club he supported as a boy.
Having failed to make a single top-flight appearance in an injury interrupted campaign with Fulham, the midfielder feels he has unfinished business where the top tier of English football is concerned.

"We all want to be there (the Premier League) - that's the bottom line," he said.

"Of course there's a lot of pressure, but personally I love hearing the owners and the fans talking about QPR returning to the Premier League one day, because as a fan and a player, that's where I want us to be.

"We know we've got the quality within the squad to get there - and we're not just talking about the play-offs; we feel we've got the strength in depth to mount a real charge next season."

Cook pinpoints long-term injuries to key players as the reason behind the R's inconsistent form last season, commenting:

"We were chatting about it at the end of the season," he recalls. "There were about ten of us in there receiving treatment and we had a laugh and a joke about it.

"But in all seriousness, when we looked around, the room was brimming with top quality players and that was the story of our season.

"We lost key players throughout - from Viney last year, to Akos and Rowly, and then the lads who were missing for three or four weeks here and there.

"No one can argue the fact that injuries played a crucial role and if we can have a little bit more luck on our side this season, we'll be firing on all cylinders, I've got no doubts about that."

SUBSCRIBE

Show your support with QPR: The Official Magazine

FILL IN THE CORRECT FORM BELOW AND POST TO:
Loftus Road Stadium, South Africa Road, Shepherds Bush, London, W12 7PJ

To subscribe to issues 2-5, tick here ☐
To subscribe to issues 3-6, tick here ☐

Delivery Details [BLOCK CAPITALS PLEASE]

Mr/Mrs/Ms/Miss   Name:
Surname:
Address:

Country: Postcode:
Telephone: Client Ref No.
Email:

ANNUAL SUBSCRIPTION FORM

☐ UK - £14.99   ☐ Europe - £23.99
☐ North America - £26.99   ☐ ROW - £33.99
☐ I enclose a cheque payable to QPR Holdings Limited.

Please Debit My

☐ Visa   ☐ Mastercard   ☐ Switch   ☐ Others
Card No ☐☐☐☐ ☐☐☐☐ ☐☐☐☐ ☐☐☐☐
Expiry Date ☐☐ ☐☐   Issue No. (Switch only) ☐☐
Sec No ☐☐☐

Address of cardholder:

Signature: Date:

DIRECT DEBIT FORM

Instruction to pay by Direct Debit. Please return completed form to QPR Holdings Ltd, Loftus Road Stadium, South Africa Road, London, W12 7PJ

Name and address of your Bank or Building Society
To: The Manager
Bank/Building Society:
Address:

Postcode:
Name of Accountholder(s)

Branch Sort Code: Account Number:

Originators Identification Number: 2 4 6 8 7 4
Reference (official use only)
Instructions to your Bank or Building Society: Please pay QPR Holdings Limited direct debits from the account detailed in this instruction subject to the safeguards assured by the direct debit guarantee. I understand that this instruction may remain with QPR Holdings Limited and if so, details will be passed electronically to my Bank/Building Society.

Signature: Date:

Banks and Building Societies may not accept Direct Debit Instructions for some types of account

This guarantee should be detached and retained by the Payer

The Direct Debit Guarantee
• This guarantee is offered by all Banks and Building Societies that take part in the Direct Debit scheme.
  The efficiency and security of the scheme is monitored and protected by your own Bank or Building Society.
• If the amounts to be paid or the payment dates change, QPR Holdings Ltd will notify you fourteen working days
  in advance of your account being debited or as otherwise agreed.
• If an error is made by QPR Holdings Ltd or your Bank or Building Society, you are guaranteed a full and immediate refund from your branch of the amount paid.
• You can cancel a Direct Debit at any time by writing to your Bank or Building Society. Please also send a copy of your letter to us.

THE RETURN OF THE MENACE...

BUY YOURS NOW!

Visit the
QPR Superstore,
call **0870 240 4547**
or go to:
www.shop.qpr.co.uk

GOALS OF THE SEASON

JORDI LÓPEZ
QPR 2-1 Bristol City
Saturday 21st March 2009
Rangers overcame fellow promotion hopefuls Bristol City helped by a first goal in blue and white hoops from Spaniard Jordi López – and what a strike it was too, leaving City custodian Basso absolutely no chance with his breathtaking 25 yard free kick.

MARTIN ROWLANDS
QPR 1-0 Wolves
Saturday 6th December 2008
Eventual winner of 'Goal of the Season', Martin Rowlands returned to the side in front of the Sky Sports' cameras against top of the table Wolverhampton Wanderers.

After dominating the first half the Super Hoops took the lead on 63 minutes when skipper Rowlands unleashed an unstoppable 25 yard strike that left Wolves keeper Hennessey clutching at thin air. It was to prove the only goal of the game and was not only a worthy match winner but also deserving of the 'Goal of the Season' award.

DAMION STEWART
Aston Villa 0-1 QPR
September 24th 2008

Damion Stewart's 58th minute header was decisive as Rangers showed their undoubted class on one of the biggest stages of them all. The Jamaican international climbed highest to notch the winner on a memorable night for the West London club and sent the 2,500 travelling R's home in raptures.

FITZ HALL
QPR 2-1 Barnsley
Saturday 9th August 2008

An early contender for 'Goal of the Season', Fitz Hall had just scored his first goal in QPR colours to level the match at 1-1 with a simple tap in however, there was nothing simple about his second effort just two minutes later. The giant centre-half spun acrobatically on the edge of the box to volley home a stunning match winner and the unlikely hero could have bagged a hat-trick if he had converted his second half spot kick.

SAMUEL DI CARMINE
QPR 1-0 Birmingham City
Tuesday 28th October 2008

Ten man Rangers toppled high flying Birmingham City thanks to Di Carmine's 54th minute wonder strike.
Despite awful conditions the R's front man collected a through ball from Tommasi and thumped in a 25 yard rocket to ensure the Super Hoops were worthy winners.

29

PLAYER OF THE SEASON

R'S DEFENDER DAMION STEWART REIGNED SUPREME AT THE CLUB'S ANNUAL PLAYER OF THE YEAR AWARDS FOR SEASON 2008/09

The giant Jamaican defender pipped fellow defender Kaspars Gorkss and goalkeeper Radek Cerny to both the Supporters' Player of the Year and the Ray Jones Players' Player of the Year awards.

Over 500 Rangers supporters were in attendance, on a night when England Under-21 international defender Matthew Connolly scooped the Daphne Biggs Supporters' Young Player of the Year award.

R's Club Captain Martin Rowlands picked up the Kiyan Prince Goal of the Season award for his stunning strike against Wolverhampton Wanderers in December, while Gareth Ainsworth was rewarded for his excellent work in the community by scooping the Community Commitment award.

R's fan Fred Perry received the Supporter of the Year accolade.

Stewart was an incredibly worthy recipient of the top two awards.

A near ever-present throughout the campaign, the Jamaican international was a commanding presence at the heart of the R's back four.

Dependable and consistent regardless of his partner at centre-back, the former Bradford City man also bagged the all-important match-winning goal against Aston Villa in the R's magnificent Carling Cup third round victory at Villa Park.

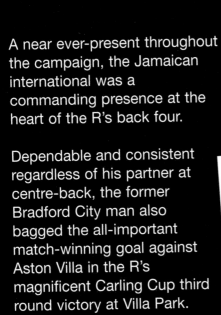

FORMER MANAGERS

```
S I H E I S K O E N X B
W M I R H D S T O N C N
Y H I A I O E T A L N A
W S G T U C L W I H S Y
A S N S H H B L N O I U
D E A B G E A Y O R C B
D E U W H R N N T W N J
O H B U R T E N S H A W
C I Y U T Y V G U G R Y
K O D I C A N I O A F O
S N I K L I W O H R T N
N O T X E S I B L E Y N
```

ANSWERS p60

Burtenshaw	Sibley	Di Canio	Smith	Docherty
Francis	Venables	Gregory	Waddock	Holloway
Houston	Wilkins	Jago	Sousa	Sexton

QPR LEGENDS

```
E A M B R E L G R A D S L
E S E O R G A S E S S K U
R I E W G L E I D S W N D
A N P L L I I N E I L O L
L T N E M E L C O F N D A
R O N S F T E L R E G E W
S N M I E E B A A L I Y A
A E T D N A N I D R E F E
M L H F W C N R R R H D S K
O L S H I T T U Y C G E I
H A R S C A C L B B H I M
T P A R K E S U R A Z A L
N O M C A A R E C B E E M
```

ANSWERS p60

Allen	Bircham	Bowles	Byrne
Clement	Currie	Fenwick	Ferdinand
Francis	Gallen	Gillard	Lazarus
Marsh	Parkes	Roeder	Shittu
Sinclair	Sinton	Thomas	Wegerle

WAYNE ROUTLEDGE

MIKELE LEIGERTWOOD

SPOT THE DIFFERENCE

There are eight differences between the photographs, how many can you spot?

SPOT THE BALL

Take a look at this action shot of Lee Cook going in for a challenge in the fixture against Plymouth Argyle at Loftus Road at the tail end of the 2008/2009 campaign. Can you spot where the ball should be?

ANSWERS p61

QPR HISTORY

HOW IT ALL BEGAN

Queens Park Rangers were formed in 1882 by the old boys of Droop Street Board School.

The boys were members of the St Jude's Institute using this as the Club Headquarters, and in the early days were known as St Judes.

The club obtained the name of Queens Park Rangers when they merged with a team called Christchurch Rangers in 1886. They called themselves Queens Park Rangers because most of the players came from the district of Queens Park.

The club's proper playing pitch was on a piece of waste ground near Kensal Rise Athletic Ground and shortly afterwards they moved to Welfords Field at a rent of £8 a year.

In 1888 they rented the London Scottish Ground at Brondesbury for £20 and it was in this year the Club first started charging for admission.

QPR changed their colours in 1892 to green and white hoops and joined the West London League. The clubs first honours soon followed, when they won The West London Observer Cup, beating Fulham 3-2 in the final.

In 1894/95 QPR won the London Cup and also entered the FA Cup for the first time.

Turning professional on December 28th 1898, QPR aimed to stop their players going to other clubs.

They played their first professional League match on 9th September at Tottenham and lost 1-0.

1961 TEAM

TONY INGHAM
(1950-1963)

Nobody has represented Queens Park Rangers more times than Tony Ingham did. The Yorkshire-born left-back enjoyed a 13 year stint with the R's and for almost a decade was an ever-present in the team. QPR took him on in June 1950 for the princely sum of £5,000. He made his debut for Rangers during a 2-1 defeat to Doncaster in November 1950, making 23 starts during his first season at Loftus Road. He added another 18 appearances before finally nailing the left-back spot down in 1952/53 with 46 starts and a truly rare goal- his first for the club- in a 4-2 loss at Crystal Palace. Ingham was 28 by the start of the 1953/54 campaign and was clearly a late bloomer- he became an integral member of the team during the mid-fifties and from February 1955 to September 1961, he didn't miss a single game- an incredible run of 250 consecutive league starts! He was 38 by the time he played during a 3-1 defeat at home to Coventry- his 548th start for the R's- a record that will take some beating.

1913 TEAM

GOALS, GOALS, GOALS

QPR's record victory came on December 3rd, 1960 when Tranmere Rovers were put to the sword during a Division Three clash at Loftus Road. Rangers won 9-2 to eclipse an 8-1 hammering of Bristol Rovers during a 1937 FA Cup tie. QPR came within one goal of setting a new record in 1983 with another 8-1 win, this time against Crewe Alexander in the League Cup- each victory remains a club record in each competition.

BRIAN BEDFORD

Few QPR strikers have struck fear into opposing defenders in quite the same way as predator supreme Brian Bedford who notched an astonishing 161 goals in 258 appearances during his time at Loftus Road. This tally ensured the Welsh forward's name was written into the club's history books before he was sold in 1965.

RODNEY MARSH

Rodney Marsh's fantastic 44 goal haul during the 1966/67 season is a record that has stood for more than 40 years and will prove difficult to beat. Rodney Marsh - perhaps the club's most popular player ever was the first person to make the number 10 shirt special. He had everything- skill, flair and an abundance of natural ability yet cost the club a mere £15,000 from Fulham. Marsh may be known best for his superb individual goal which forced extra time in Rangers' historic 3-2 win in the League Cup over West Brom back in 1967.

THE FOOTBALL LEAGUE

CUP FINAL

QUEEN'S PARK RANGERS
VERSUS
WEST BROMWICH ALBION
(HOLDERS)

SATURDAY MARCH 4th, 1967
Kick-off 3.30 p.m.

EMPIRE STADIUM WEMBLEY
OFFICIAL PROGRAMME — ONE SHILLING
Incorporating Special Cup Final Issue of Football League Review

GODDARD

Legendary striker George Goddard is the club's leading career goal-scorer with 172 league goals. The greatest goal-scorer in QPR's history, Goddard was a goal machine that wrote his name into the club's record books with his incredible predatory instincts over a seven year period. He hit his peak in the late 1920s, and passed the 100 goals milestone in under three and a half seasons with the R's.

RECORDS

ATTENDANCE 35,353 v Leeds United, Division One, 27th April 1973

VICTORY
9-2 v Tranmere Rovers, Division Three, 3rd December 1960
8-1 v Bristol Rovers, FA Cup, 27th November 1937
8-1 v Crewe Alexandra, League Cup, 3rd October 1983

DEFEAT
1-8 v Mansfield Town, Division Three, 15th March 1965
1-8 v Manchester United, Division One, 19th March 1969

MOST GOALS IN ONE SEASON 44 – Rodney Marsh 1966/67

MOST CAREER GOALS 189 – George Goddard

MOST CAPPED PLAYER 52 Caps, Alan McDonald, Northern Ireland

RECORD TRANSFER RECEIVED
£6m Les Ferdinand – to Newcastle United 1995

YOUNGEST PLAYER TO REPRESENT QPR
Frank Sibley, 15 years, 275 days old

OLDEST PLAYER TO REPRESENT QPR
Ray Wilkins, 39 years, 352 days old

ALLEN FAMILY

No family has contributed more to Queens Park Rangers Football Club than the Allens; Les, Clive, Martin and Bradley. All four men enjoyed significant careers at Loftus Road, and Clive (son of Les), enjoyed two stints in W12 during the late seventies and early eighties. The young Rangers number 9, helped the R's to an FA Cup final in 1982 and to a Second Division title a year later. His record of 83 goals in 158 games, whilst in West London is nothing short of incredible.

EUROPE

QPR have entered European competitions only twice but both times have left lasting memories. The Hoops progressed to the quarter finals in 1976 by beating some of the best teams in Europe at the time, but exited on a penalty shootout away to Greek side AEK Athens.

In 1984/85 Rangers qualified again but due to having an artificial pitch had to play Home ties at Highbury.

After getting past Reykjavik, over two legs the R's bowed out on away goals to Partizan Belgrade.

FA CUP

There is only one season that Rangers really threatened to lift the FA Cup and that was during the 1981/82 campaign when the club went all the way to the final as a Division Two side. The Hoops battled well against their first division opponents Tottenham Hotspur, and had Peter Hucker to thank for a string of fine saves to keep the score at 0-0 after half time. Glenn Hoddle's deflected drive put Spurs ahead on 109 minutes, and all seemed lost for Terry Venables' side, until Bob Hazells' nod on from a Stainrod throw in, was headed home by Terry Fenwick with just five minutes left, forcing a replay.

FOOTBALL ASSOCIATION CHALLENGE CUP COMPETITION

CUP FINAL

SATURDAY 22nd MAY, 1982 KICK OFF 3.00p.m.

QUEENS PARK RANGERS
V
TOTTENHAM HOTSPUR

OFFICIAL SOUVENIR PROGRAMME 80p.

Wembley

Though Rangers dominated the replay and were denied by a combination of the woodwork and a defiant Ray Clemence, a Glenn Hoddle penalty was enough to deny the Hooped Heros from W12.

WEST LONDON CLASSIC ENCOUNTERS

CRUNCH

Oh brother,

RANGERS DELIGHT FOR SEXTON

CHELSEA 0, QUEEN'S PARK RANGERS 3

DAVE SEXTON was delighted, but he wouldn't let it show. Gloating is not his style.

"I was nervous," he admitted, as though embarrassed by the completeness of his comeback.

Sacked by Chelsea three months ago, his return to Stamford Bridge as manager of Queen's Park Rangers had turned out to be a triumph.

"It was like a player going back to face a club who gave him a free transfer," he said. "There was something to prove."

The proof came with the sudden excellence of the Rangers' football in the second half.

They scored three times and left Chelsea's defence in ruins.

But not before referee Bob Matthewson had been stretched to the limits of his patience by the seamier side of British football.

Criticism

"The worst referee we have had this season," muttered someone in Chelsea's tea room at half-time. It was a common complaint.

The criticism ignored a constant flow of fouls and bickering back-chat.

Mr. Matthewson wasn't always right. Referees rarely are. You take the good with the bad which is what the players were not prepared to do.

"Cool it," instructed both managers at half-time.

Cool it they did, but not before referee Matthewson had rightly booked Clement and Francis, of Rangers, and Chelsea's Droy and Harris.

By then, Parkes had kept Rangers going with a collection of outstanding saves as Chelsea surged forward with a wicked wind at their backs.

Kember, Garland and Wilkins will all support Chelsea manager Ron Suart's opinion that Parkes, on his day is as good as there is.

Losing Hutchinson with a back strain didn't help Chelsea's cause and if Kember at half speed their were suddenly there to be taken.

By Ken Jones

The damage was done on the floor by lively, intelligent running at the heart of a leaden-footed defence.

But first it was Francis with a shot from nowhere in the fiftieth minute who sickened Chelsea.

He found the top far corner of Phillips' goal with an angled twenty-five yarder.

A linesman's flag delayed the jubilation, but only for a second or two. Referee Matthewson knew a good thing when he saw it.

Within two minutes Givens flat-footed Hay and the cumbersome Droy to strike Beck's pass low and left-footed for the second.

He was six inches away from another barely a minute later.

But it was Givens who got the third, running Bowles' fine pass beyond Phillips to squeeze a shot through the legs of three defenders.

"A game of two halves," said Chelsea manager Suart. The right one belonged to Sexton.

Man of the match: Phil Parkes (Q.P.R).

CHELSEA: Phillips, Locke, Harris, Hollins, Droy, Hay, Kember, Wilkins, Garland, Hutchinson, Cooke. Sub: Houseman.

Q.P.R.: Parkes, Clement, Gillard, Masson, McLintock, Webb, Thomas, Francis, Beck, Bowles, Givens. Sub: Shanks.

REF: R. Matthewson (Bolton).

BATTLE STATIONS

It looks like the battle of Stamford Bridge as Chelsea and QPR players get into the action. The only thing missing is the ball. But who cares about a little thing like that? Stan Bowles, obviously. He's sitting pretty with a 3—0 smile on his face.

Busby turns the relegation screw on Chelsea

SUPER SUB

CHELSEA 1, QUEENS PARK RANGERS 3

SUBSTITUTE Martyn Busby appeared like a fairy godmother to guide Rangers to their first win of 1979 — and offer a ray of hope in their relegation struggle.

With the match poised at 1—1, Busby made his entrance on the hour and set up Glenn Roeder's goal five minutes later.

Then he sealed this grim battle for First Division survival with a goal of his own in the 74th minute.

From Chelsea's view-

By Pat Needham

point, this was surely one of the final nails in their coffin. On St. Patrick's Day of all days, Chelsea manager Danny Blanchflower was entitled to expect a little luck. But it didn't work out that way.

"It wasn't a good day for us, was it?" he said. "We need a lot of luck to stay up and we're just not getting it at the moment."

It was no surprise when the 23rd minute.

Rangers took the lead in the 23rd minute. Chelsea defender Nutten lost the ball, then failed to make a convincing challenge on Goddard, who slipped the ball past Borota.

As Ray Wilkins found his touch, Chelsea began to buzz. In the 35th minute Wilkins found Stanley on the right and his cross was pushed past his own keeper by Shanks, as he rushed back to clear.

For a while Chelsea looked the likelier side. But after Docherty wasted an open goal chance from only five yards out a must leading to his replacement by sub Langley stepped in to steal the show.

Man of the match: Ray Wilkins (Chelsea).

● Rangers manager Steve Burtenshaw missed the match. He was in the Midlands trying to clinch the £100,000 signing of West Brom winger Willie Johnston.

CHELSEA 0, QUEEN'S

DAVE SEXTON w
wouldn't let it sho
tyle.

"I was nervous," he a
rrased by the completene
Sack by Chelsea three
onth o, his return to
amford Bridge as man-
er of Queen's Park

By Ken Jones

BLUE MURDER

Gary's glitter

HAT-TRICK hero Gary Bannister outjumps the Chelsea defence to head his second goal yesterday. Picture: BRENDAN MONKS

By NIGEL CLARKE

Rangers run riot

QPR 6, Chelsea 0

CHELSEA'S dream that they could bring the championship to Stamford Bridge was hit for six yesterday.

They were beaten out of sight by Rangers and the surrender came just two days after being outplayed at home by West Ham.

The stark facts are they have now conceded ten goals in two devastating defeats.

Their misery was multiplied when David Speedie was sent off for

the second time this season in the 67th minute after an elbow incident that floored Ian Dawes.

Now the fiery Scottish striker faces his third suspension of the season.

From the moment they fell behind in the ninth minute, Chelsea were a shambles.

The Blues had never previously been beaten on Rangers' plastic

pitch, but this time they were humiliated by a side who put on a show-piece of soccer.

Manager John Hollins put a brave face on when he said: "It's been a very bad Easter for us, but I'm not conceding the championship."

Chelsea were destroyed by some quality finishing that brought

Bannister could have

Gary Bannister a hat-trick, his first goals for 11 weeks.

Bannister opened the floodgates by cutting the ball across the despairing Steve Francis from the narrowest of angles.

And it was the centre forward who got the second in the 25th minute, heading home with Francis rooted on his line.

got his hat-trick with two more efforts, one from a brilliant Terry Fenwick free kick, before John Bryne got the goal of the game in the 44th minute.

He beat four defenders in a 40-yard run that belonged to the days of Rodney Marsh, before sending Francis the wrong way.

Bannister completed his hat-trick in the 58th minute and set-up Bryne for his second six minutes later.

Then with just eight minutes to go, substitute Leroy Rosenior cut through a wide open defence for number six.

Published by Mirror Group Newspapers 1986. Printed by...

FULHAM'S MISERY

By HARRY MILLER

QPR 3, Fulham 1

FULHAM fell out of the promotion frame for the first time in six months yesterday as Rangers got the win that guarantees them the Second Division championship.

While the celebration champagne flowed for Rangers, the news for Fulham was all bad.

Midfielder Ray Lewington was sent off for a foul on Simon Stainrod a minute from time, and Leicester's draw at Leeds means they now need Fulham on goal difference, with two games each to go.

Fulham face Carlisle at home and Derby away, while Leicester go to Oldham and then meet Burnley at Filbert Street.

After seeing his side devoured by the Ranger's flowing football, manager Malcolm Macdonald admitted: "We've got to win our last two games and look for a slip-up by Leicester.

"I still think we are good enough to go up.

"We should have had two penalties here — when Gordon Davies was tripped in the first half, and Bob Hazell handled on the line after the interval.

"Lewington has never gone in to foul intentionally.

"It was something entirely out of character today. He was genuinely going for the ball, but there was also a bit of frustration about a deci-

sion which has just gone against him."

Fulham moved into the top three last November. But nerves have clearly got to Macdonald's young team, despite his efforts to calm the tension.

Rangers scored in the fifth minute, played some exhilarating stuff, and never allowed Fulham to settle.

As manager Terry Venables said: "Fulham are a good side, but we took them by the throat and made it difficult for them to play."

The goal John Gregory shot after five minutes

was described by Venables as "one to compare with anything we have scored this season."

The First Division looked further and further away for Fulham when Stainrod played the ball in for Sealy to make it 2-0 in the 11th minute.

Five minutes into the second half, Stainrod put Rangers three up.

Fulham brought on substitute John Reeves and improved considerably.

But the goal Davies skilfully shot 20 minutes from the end was too little, too late.

Lewington sent off as promotion bid fades

	P	W	D	L	F	A	Pts
QPR	39	25	6	8	73	32	81
Wolves	40	20	14	6	65	40	74
Leicester	40	19	9	12	70	43	66
Fulham	40	19	9	12	62	48	66
Newc'tle	39	16	12	11	66	50	60
Sheff. W.	40	15	15	10	57	44	60

HOPE: Fulham manager Malcolm Macdonald and assistant Ray Harford confident.

DESPAIR: Macdonald and Harford can't bear to watch as Rangers ram in three goals.

HAPPINESS: Tony Sealy jumps into Gary Waddock's arms after scoring Rangers' second goal in the 11th minute. Pictures: MONTE FRESCO

43

PLAYER PROFILES

1. LEE CAMP
BORN: 22-08-84
POSITION: GOALKEEPER

Lee Camp joined QPR from Derby County for a fee of £300,000 in the summer of 2007.

The former England Under-21 goalkeeper made five appearances in all competitions for the R's last season, before spending a successful loan spell at Nottingham Forest.

Camp appeared in 15 league fixtures for the Reds, helping them stave off relegation from the second tier.

2. DAMIEN DELANEY
BORN: 20-07-81
POSITION: DEFENDER

Former Hull City left-back Damien Delaney penned a three-and-a-half year deal with the R's in January 2008.

After impressing during his first six months in W12, Delaney went on to enjoy a productive second season in the Blue and White Hoops.

The Republic of Ireland international made 35 starts in the Championship, scoring one league goal, and also netted in the R's Carling Cup victory against Swindon Town.

3. DAMION STEWART

BORN: 18-08-80
POSITION: DEFENDER

Jamaican international Damion Stewart joined the R's in the summer of 2006.

After a steady, if unspectacular start, Stewart was a virtual ever-present in his first campaign in W12 and then went on to enjoy a productive second season at Loftus Road.

But it was last season - his third full campaign at this level - that saw Stewart's performances reach new heights, with the giant defender bagging four goals in all competitions, including the crucial winner against Aston Villa.

His displays at the heart of the Rangers back four secured him a notable end of season double, as he was named Supporters' Player and Player's Player of the Year.

5. FITZ HALL

BORN: 20-12-80
POSITION: DEFENDER

Fitz Hall penned a four-and-a-half year deal with Rangers at the start of the 2008 January transfer window.

The defender, who gained vast Premiership experience during spells at Wigan Athletic and Crystal Palace, suffered his fair share of injuries last term, and coupled with the emergence of Kaspars Gorkss, was restricted to just 27 appearances in all competitions.

4. GAVIN MAHON

BORN: 02-01-77
POSITION: MIDFIELDER

Midfielder Gavin Mahon joined QPR in January 2008 from local rivals Watford.

A solid and reliable midfield general, Mahon - who skippered former Club Watford to the Premiership during a five-year spell at Vicarage Road - made 40 appearances in all competitions last term.

During that spell, he also wore the skipper's armband, in the absence of regular Club Captain, Martin Rowlands.

7. WAYNE ROUTLEDGE
BORN: 07-01-85
POSITION: MIDFIELDER

Diminutive wide-man Wayne Routledge joined QPR from Premiership outfit Aston Villa in January 2009.

Rangers had to beat off stiff competition from Cardiff City, amongst others, to land his prized signature, after the midfielder impressed during his nine match stay at Ninian Park.

Routledge went on to enjoy a productive first few months in W12, making 19 appearances and scoring a solitary goal, against Derby County in mid-January.

6. MIKELE LEIGERTWOOD
BORN: 12-11-82
POSITION: MIDFIELDER

Rangers completed the signing of no-nonsense midfielder Mikele Leigertwood on the final day of the 2007 summer transfer window.

The Sheffield United ace put pen to paper on a three-year deal, after the two Clubs agreed an undisclosed fee for his services.

Leigertwood went on to play a crucial role during his first season at Loftus Road, scoring a creditable five goals in 40 league appearances, and was a mainstay in the R's midfield last season too.
The no-nonsense midfielder made 46 appearances in all competitions, scoring two goals.

8. ROWAN VINE
BORN: 21-09-82
POSITION: STRIKER

Queens Park Rangers completed the signing of Birmingham City front-man Rowan Vine in January 2008.

The experienced front-man signed a four-and-a-half year contract, after a successful loan period in W12.

Vine went on to bag three crucial goals in 15 appearances during his first season at Loftus Road, prior to sustaining a fractured leg during a freak training ground accident in early April.

That injury restricted his involvement last season, with the striker returning for the final few weeks of the campaign, scoring one goal in five appearances.

10. AKOS BUZSAKY
BORN: 07-05-82
POSITION: MIDFIELDER

A player with outstanding individual ability, Akos Buzsaky made an immediate impact following his move to W12 from fellow Championship outfit Plymouth Argyle.

The Hungarian international, who initially joined on loan prior to making the deal permanent in January 2008, scored six goals in his first 13 appearances, and ended the campaign with ten goals to his name.

Buzsaky's taste for the spectacular also saw him scoop the Kiyan Prince Goal of the Season award, but his first full season in W12 proved to be a frustrating one, with the talented ace notching just a solitary goal in his five league starts.

The midfielder suffered an Anterior Cruciate Ligament injury in the R's Carling Cup tie against Manchester United in November, which ruled him out for the remainder of the season.

9. DEXTER BLACKSTOCK
BORN: 20-05-86
POSITION: STRIKER

QPR added to their attacking options by completing the signing of Southampton striker Dexter Blackstock, for an undisclosed fee, in August 2006.

The hardworking front-man bagged 14 goals in all competitions in his maiden season at the Club and was deservedly named Young Player of the Year.

Six goals followed a year later, before the striker suffered a frustrating 2008/09 campaign.

In a season which included a loan spell at Nottingham Forest, Blackstock finished the campaign with 14 goals to his name.

11. PATRICK AGYEMANG
BORN: 29-09-80
POSITION: STRIKER

Patrick Agyemang joined QPR from Preston in January 2008 on a four-and-a-half year deal, after the two Clubs agreed an undisclosed fee for his services.

The Ghanaian international enjoyed a honeymoon period to remember for the R's, bagging eight goals in his first six league appearances.

Agyemang went on to score nine goals in all competitions, but injury struck last season.

The former Wimbledon man was restricted to just over 20 appearances in all competitions, scoring two goals, including one against his former Club Preston on the final day of the season.

13. KASPARS GORKSS
BORN: 06-11-81
POSITION: DEFENDER

Rangers ended their search for a centre half with the capture of Kaspars Gorkss in July 2008.

The Latvian international put pen to paper on a three year deal, after the R's agreed an undisclosed fee with Blackpool for his services.

And the giant defender - after a mixed start to life in W12 - went on to enjoy a profitable maiden season at Loftus Road, making 35 appearances in all competitions, and finishing runner-up in both the Player's Player and Supporters' Player of the Year awards.

14. MARTIN ROWLANDS
BORN: 08-02-79
POSITION: MIDFIELDER

Hammersmith-born midfielder Martin Rowlands joined Rangers in July 2003 on a free transfer from local rivals Brentford.

An outstanding 2007/08 campaign saw the midfielder named Players' Player of the Year and after a four-year absence from the international fold, Rowlands was recalled to the full Republic of Ireland squad under new Eire boss Giovanni Trapattoni.

But his 2009/10 campaign failed to hit such heights, with an Anterior Cruciate Ligament injury – sustained against Derby County in January - ruling him out for the season.

However, he still featured in the end of season awards, with his sublime strike against Wolverhampton Wanderers sealing the coveted Kiyan Prince Goal of the Season crown.

16. MATTHEW CONNOLLY
BORN: 24-09-87
POSITION: DEFENDER

Matthew Connolly penned a three-and-a-half year deal with the R's in January 2008.

A product of the successful Arsenal academy, Connolly went on to make 21 appearances in all competitions for Rangers in his first six months at the Club.

Those displays led to a deserved call up to Stuart Pearce's England Under-21 squad and the versatile defender has excelled ever since.

Connolly made 39 appearances for the R's in the 2008/9 term, and was rightly named Supporters' Young Player of the Year.

15. PETER RAMAGE
BORN: 22-11-83
POSITION: DEFENDER

A versatile and committed defender, Peter Ramage joined QPR on a free transfer from Newcastle United in the summer of 2008.

The Ashington-born defender - who made 51 starts for his boyhood Club prior to his move to Loftus Road - went from strength to strength in his first season with the R's, making 34 appearances in all competitions and consistently performing to a very high standard at right-back.

19. ANGELO BALANTA
BORN: 01-07-90
POSITION: FORWARD

Teenage striker Angelo Balanta put pen-to-paper on his first professional contract with the R's in January 2008.

The teenage Colombian, who made three First Team appearances in his time as an Under-18 player, inked a deal that keeps him at the Club until the summer of 2010.

After scoring in the R's Carling Cup victory against Swindon Town at the start of the 2008/09 season, Balanta excelled during a loan spell at Wycombe Wanderers, before returning to W12 for the final few months of the campaign.

17. LEE COOK
BORN: 03-08-82
POSITION: MIDFIELDER

R's fans favourite Lee Cook rejoined Rangers on loan from Fulham in August 2008.

The left sided midfielder, who joined the Cottagers just 12 months earlier, was named both Player's Player and Supporter's Player of the Year prior to his departure to the West London outfit.

But an injury-interrupted spell at Craven Cottage eventually led to his return to W12, and after making his loan deal permanent in January 2009, Cook went on to make 38 appearances in all competitions last term and scored a stunning free-kick against Charlton Athletic on Boxing Day.

21. MATTEO ALBERTI
BORN: 04-08-88
POSITION: MIDFIELDER

Brescia-born midfielder Matteo Alberti joined the R's in the summer of 2008 from Chievo.

The Italian, who is equally adept on either flank, made six starts in the Championship in his maiden season in England, including a fixture against Nottingham Forest, which saw him net a stunning brace in a 2-2 draw.

25. HOGAN EPHRAIM
BORN: 31-03-88
POSITION: MIDFIELDER

After a successful loan spell in W12, winger Hogan Ephraim signed a three-and-a-half year contract with QPR in January 2008.

The diminutive winger made 30 appearances in all competitions in 2007/08, scoring two goals and proved what a valuable, versatile asset he is to the R's side again last term.

The midfielder scored a stunning third goal in our 3-0 demolition of Blackpool, as the former England Youth product excelled in a more central role.

24. RADEK CERNY
BORN: 18-02-74
POSITION: GOALKEEPER

Goalkeeper Radek Cerny joined the R's in the summer of 2008.

The former Tottenham Hotspur and Slavia Prague stopper arrived in W12 with a terrific track record and duly went on to make the number one jersey his own.

Cerny was a mainstay in the R's side throughout the 2008/09 campaign, making 47 appearances in all competitions, and inspiring Rangers to one of the best defensive records in the Championship.

26. GARETH AINSWORTH
BORN: 10-05-73
POSITION: MIDFIELDER

Fans' favourite Gareth Ainsworth joined QPR after being released from Cardiff City in June 2003.

The bustling midfielder's contribution to the Rangers cause has been without question ever since, providing leadership and guile, as well as priceless assists and match-winning goals.

Despite two serious injuries during the 2006/07 campaign, Ainsworth returned stronger than ever last season, making 25 appearances in all competitions.

After a brief stint assisting former Manager Luigi De Canio, the experienced midfielder was handed a player / coach role by former boss Iain Dowie in the summer of 2008.

Ainsworth went on to enjoy two stints as Caretaker boss, as well as working under ex-gaffer Paulo Sousa.

27. HEIDAR HELGUSON
BORN: 22-08-77
POSITION: STRIKER

QPR rescued Iceland international Helguson from Bolton Wanderers after the former Watford man fell out of favour under then-Manager Gary Megson.

Initially signed on a loan deal, he made the move to W12 permanent as soon as the transfer window opened in January 2009.

Three goals in seven appearances indicated a man relieved to be back playing, and he has added a new dimension to the Rangers attack with tireless work rate and phenomenal aerial prowess.

Helguson went on to finish the campaign with five goals in 21 appearances in all competitions.

29. GARY BORROWDALE
BORN: 16-07-85
POSITION: DEFENDER

Former England Under-21 defender Gary Borrowdale joined the R's from Coventry City in January 2009.

However, his first six months in W12 proved to be frustrating, with the defender spending most of that time on loan at League One outfit Brighton & Hove Albion.

RADEK CERNY

53

THE BIG QUIZ

1 Who was denied a hat-trick against Barnsley on the opening game of the Season?

2 Which Midlands club did Damion Stewart score against to get us through to a mouthwatering tie against Manchester United in the Carling Cup?

3 How many points off the play-offs were we at the end of the 08/09 season?

4 What team did we go 2-0 down against at home but came back to win 3-2?

5 Who came off against Manchester United away in the 1-0 defeat in the Carling Cup and remained sidelined for the rest of the campaign?

6 Who scored his first hat-trick of his career against Carlisle United in the Carling Cup?

7 Who did Dexter Blackstock make a loan move to until the end of the season?

8 What team did QPR beat 2-0 away when Martin Rowlands was stretchered off and effectively, ended his season early?

9 What team did Jordi López score his blinder of a free-kick against, marking his first goal for the R's?

10 Who scored QPR's goal of the season in a well deserved 1-0 win?

11 Who did QPR sign Liam Miller from?

12 Which player had the most appearances for the Super Hoops in 08/09?

13 Who did Wayne Routledge come to QPR from?

14 Which two players celebrated their 21st birthdays during the season?

15 Which championship manager, who did the double over QPR in season 08/09, is now at the helm of the Loftus Road Club?

16 At what game did Wayne Routledge make his debut QPR appearance?

17 How many points did QPR finish the season with?

18 Where in the League did QPR finish?

19 Against whom did Rowan Vine score his only goal of the season?

20 How many games did the final score finish 0-0?

21 How many clean sheets did Radek Cerny keep in the League and Cup Competitions?

22 Who was QPR's first defeat of the season to?

23 How many games did we win this season?

24 What was our biggest win of the season and who was the opposition?

25 How many red cards were shown to QPR players?

26 How many penalties did we concede?

27 In which winter month did we not register a win?

28 Which player had the most shots on target?

29 Which two players had the most assists during the season?

30 Who did QPR get on loan from Coventry City in November?

ON 'R' TRAVELS

R'S WIN VILLA THRILLER

ASTON VILLA 0, QPR 1
CARLING CUP, THIRD ROUND
WEDNESDAY 24TH SEPTEMBER 2008

Damion Stewart's second half header booked Rangers' place in the Fourth Round of the Carling Cup, on a night to remember for the Super Hoops.

The Jamaican international leapt to head home Daniel Parejo's pin-point cross, as the R's - backed by 3,500 fanatical fans - claimed the notable scalp of a Villa side sitting pretty in fourth spot in the Premiership.

Victory was no less than the R's deserved, as Villa failed to breakdown a resolute Rangers defence, led magnificently by Fitz Hall.

To a man, the Hoops out-battled and out-foxed the hosts, with Radek Cerny a virtual spectator in the R's goal.

QPR: CERNY, DELANEY, STEWART, MAHON, HALL, PAREJO, BUZSAKY (LEIGERTWOOD 82), AGYEMANG (DI CARMINE 66), ROWLANDS, CONNOLLY, LEDESMA (BALANTA 91).
SUBS: CAMP, BLACKSTOCK, GORKSS, EPHRAIM.
GOALS: STEWART (58).

QUOTES IAIN DOWIE:

"To come to a Club like this, led by a Manager like Martin O'Neill, and to win and keep a clean sheet is just unbelievable.

"Martin always manages to get the best out of his players and I'm incredibly proud that we've come here and upset the odds."

"I'm proud of each and every one of the lads and it's a really pleasing result.

"When you come to a side that can bring on a player like Gabi Agbonlahor and in my opinion they've got one of the best wingers in the game in Ashley Young, it will always cause you problems, but we coped with it really well.

"I thought we had loads of possession up until the edge of the penalty box, but we didn't use the ball well enough.

" It's a special night for us – terrific "

"We gave them such cheap giveaways and they've got blistering pace which could have really hurt us.

"But our defensive shape improved as the game went on and we got the desired result."

TEVEZ ON THE SPOT
MANCHESTER UNITED 1, QPR 0
CARLING CUP, FOURTH ROUND
TUESDAY 11TH NOVEMBER 2008

QPR exited the Carling Cup after going down 1-0 at a drenched Old Trafford, as a Carlos Tevez penalty condemned the R's to a long homeward journey.

In truth, the visitors never really threatened and were largely outplayed by their more illustrious hosts.

The R's put on a gutsy, determined defensive showing, with keeper Radek Cerny in sparkling form throughout to deny a host of United players.

But ultimately, a lack of creativity, compounded by an early injury to Akos Buzsaky, cost the R's a chance to pull off a shock victory.

QPR: CERNY, STEWART, MAHON, HALL, PAREJO (LEDESMA 46), BLACKSTOCK, BUZSAKY (AGYEMANG 33), ROWLANDS, RAMAGE, CONNOLLY, COOK (DI CARMINE 78).
SUBS: COLE, DELANEY, GORKSS, EPHRAIM.

QUOTES
GARETH AINSWORTH:

"I was so proud of the boys, as I always am.

"The passion was there - they did what we wanted them to do. We gave a good account of ourselves and we didn't get completely turned over.

"What can I say about the fans?

"They were amazing. They sang their hearts out and I'm just sorry we couldn't reward their efforts with a victory.

"Having said that, I don't think they'll have any complaints with how we performed."

LEE COOK

QUIZ ANSWERS

p32 WORD SEARCH

```
S I H E I S K O E N X B
W M I R H D S T O N C N
Y H I A I O E T A L N A
W S G T U C L W I H S Y
A S N S H H B L N O I U
D E A B G E A Y O R C B
D E U W H R N N T W N J
O H B U R T E N S H A W
C I Y U T Y V G U G R Y
K O D I C A N I O A F O
S N I K L I W O H R T N
N O T X E S I B L E Y N
```

p33 WORD SEARCH

```
E A M B R E L G R A D S L
E S E O R G A S E S S K U
R I E W G L E I D S W N D
A N P L L I N E I L O L
L T N E M E L C O F N D A
R O N S F T E I R E G E W
S N M I E E B A A L I Y A
A E T D N A N I D R E F E
M L H F W C N B R H D S K
O L S H I T T U Y C G E I
H A R S C A C L B B H I M
T P A R K E S U R A Z A L
N O M C A A R E C B E E M
```

p36 SPOT THE DIFFERENCE

p37 SPOT THE BALL

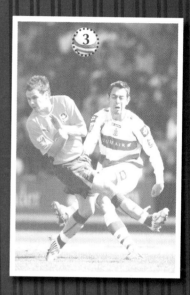

p54 THE BIG QUIZ

1	FITZ HALL	9	BRISTOL CITY	15	JIM MAGILTON	23	13
2	ASTON VILLA	10	MARTIN ROWLANDS	16	QPR V COVENTRY	24	CARLISLE UNITED, 4-0 (CARLING CUP)
3	13 POINTS	11	SUNDERLAND	17	61 POINTS	25	4
4	SHEFFIELD WEDNESDAY	12	RADEK CERNY (42)	18	11TH	26	5
5	AKOS BUZSAKY	13	ASTON VILLA	19	SHEFFIELD WEDNESDAY	27	FEBRUARY
6	LEDESMA	14	MATT CONNOLLY (24/9/1987) & HOGAN EPHRAIM (31/3/1988)	20	11 GAMES	28	DEXTER BLACKSTOCK
7	NOTTINGHAM FOREST			21	19 GAMES	29	LEE COOK & MIKELE LEIGERTWOOD
8	DERBY COUNTY			22	SHEFFIELD UNITED	30	GARY BORROWDALE

ROAD

GAVIN MAHON